ROBOTS, GADGETS, and ARTIFICIAL INTELLIGENCE

Tom Jackson

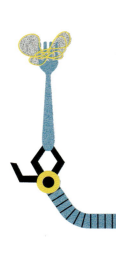

OXFORD
UNIVERSITY PRESS

OXFORD
UNIVERSITY PRESS

Great Clarendon Street, Oxford OX2 6DP

Oxford is a registered trade mark of Oxford University Press
in the UK and in certain other countries

© Oxford University Press 2022
Text written by Tom Jackson
Illustrated by Adam Quest and Ana Seixas

Designed and edited by Raspberry Books Ltd

The moral rights of the author and artist have been asserted
Database right Oxford University Press (maker)

First published 2022
This hardback edition published 2025

All rights reserved.

Library of Congress Cataloging-in-Publication Data is available.

ISBN 978-1-382-06649-5

1 3 5 7 9 10 8 6 4 2

Printed in China

The manufacturing process conforms to the
environmental regulations of the country of origin.

Acknowledgments

The publisher and authors would like to thank the following for permission to use photographs and other copyright material:

Cover: Pavlo S/Shutterstock
Photos: p1(tl): Pavlo S/Shutterstock; p6: higyou/Shutterstock; p10: public domain; p11: charles taylor/Shutterstock; p13: REUTERS/Alamy Stock Photo; p16: rcherem/Shutterstock; p18: Baloncici/Shutterstock; pp22-23: Phonlamai Photo/Shutterstock; pp24-25: Raksha Shelare/Shutterstock; p25(t): Serjio74/Shutterstock; p25(b): Richard Peterson/Shutterstock; p27: Serjio74/Shutterstock; p30: Natata/Shutterstock; p35: M.Stasy/Shutterstock; p38: PaulPaladin/Shutterstock; p44: Marzolino/Shutterstock; p45(t): IanDagnall Computing/Alamy Stock Photo; p45(b): public domain; p59: kai hecker/Shutterstock; pp62-63: Glenn Price/Shutterstock; p63: James Steidl/Shutterstock; p64(t): Bitcoin/Shutterstock; p64(b): ALX1618/Shutterstock; p69: Gorodenkoff/Shutterstock; p72(t): Chesky/Shutterstock; p72(b): Nerthuz/Shutterstock; p83: Kismet' illustration produced by Adam Quest with kind permission by MIT.; p84: ZUMA Press, Inc./Alamy Stock Photo; p86: Pressmaster/Shutterstock. **Front end paper:** pp2-3: Aleksandr Bryliaev/Shutterstock. **Back end paper:** p2: Pavlo S/Shutterstock.

Author photo courtesy of Tom Jackson.

Artwork by **Adam Quest**, **Ana Seixas**, Ekaterina Gorelova, Geraldine Sy, Raspberry Books, and Oxford University Press. 'Kismet' illustration produced by Adam Quest with kind permission of MIT.

Every effort has been made to contact copyright holders of material reproduced in this book. Any omissions will be rectified in subsequent printings if notice is given to the publisher.

Images are to be used only within the context of the pages in this book.

Did you know that we also publish Oxford's bestselling and award-winning **Very Short Introductions** series? These are perfect for adults and students
www.veryshortintroductions.com

Contents

Chapter 1. Amazing Machines — 4
Chapter 2. Going Robotic — 9
Chapter 3. What is AI? — 24
Chapter 4. How to Make AI — 34
Chapter 5. Meet the AIs — 52
Chapter 6. Smart Robots and Clever Gadgets — 62
Chapter 7. AIs and Us — 80
Glossary — 90
Index — 95

Chapter 1

Amazing Machines

Imagine a machine that can do everything that humans do. It might move around, talk, hold tools, and solve puzzles. Now imagine the same machine, or maybe many different ones, that together can do everything we need. Perhaps these machines could do anything humans do—and do some things even better!

They do the dishes, cook, build, and make repairs.

They drive the car, fly planes, look after us when we're sick, teach lessons at school, and even write books.

**AMAZING MACHINES**

Changing technology

This might sound like an idea from the future, but in fact, people have been dreaming of helpful machines like this for hundreds, even thousands, of years. All new inventions, from the wheel to the phone, were created to make life easier in some way by having a machine do a job for us.

Machines and tools are examples of **technology**. Technology is a big idea—it means that we humans use what we know about the world to invent useful things.

As we learn more about the world, we can make better, smarter inventions and **gadgets** (a gadget is any small and useful device). Once upon a time, the spoon was a new gadget, as was the window, the shoe, or pen and paper.

My Story by A. Robot

ROBOTS, GADGETS, AND ARTIFICIAL INTELLIGENCE

Today's inventors are much closer to creating the machines that do our work for us, and to get there, they are working hard on two kinds of technology: **robots** and **artificial intelligence**.

Perhaps you picture a robot as some kind of human-shaped metal machine with electric **motors** instead of muscles, and cameras for eyes. However, it is what a machine does that makes it a robot, not what it looks like.

Speak like a scientist

ROBOT

A robot is a machine that works automatically, or by itself, and is also able to pick up information that tells it when to start working, when to stop, and to adjust what it is doing for different situations. Using this description, all kinds of things can be robots. They do not need a body that looks a certain way, with arms, legs, big pincers, and lasers—although all of those things might be useful. In fact, computer programs, such as smartphone apps and websites, can be robots—or "bots" for short—and they have no body at all! Robotics is the science of building robots.

✸ Speak like a scientist ✸

ARTIFICIAL INTELLIGENCE

A useful robot needs to be smart enough to do the right things at the right time. For that, the robot needs something very special: intelligence. Generally, humans have a natural intelligence that increases as we learn about the world. A clever robot needs the same kind of thing, but we will have to make this intelligence for it. An intelligence system created by humans is called an artificial intelligence, or an AI for short. We still have a lot to learn about how to make AIs.

In this very short introduction to robots, gadgets, and artificial intelligence we are going to find out how a robot can take control of its movements to do a range of useful jobs. Plus we'll look at how an artificial intelligence is a computer system smart enough to figure out problems and make decisions—and even reorganize its own program to make itself smarter.

Inventors have been working for centuries to create new technologies and gadgets to make robots stronger and smarter—

but there is still a lot to do.

ROBOTS, GADGETS, AND ARTIFICIAL INTELLIGENCE

Read on and discover:

why robots come in all shapes and sizes, including **jellyfish** and **kangeroos**

Spot, the **dancing** robot dog

the artificially intelligent robots working on **other planets**

how **AIs** are getting even **smarter** by using the internet

Let's begin our journey into robots and AI. It will be a journey into the future.

Chapter 2

Going Robotic

Unlike humans, a robot will never get tired, scared, bored, or hungry. But it is unlikely that robots will end up doing everything for us. Instead, we will use them to do the most dangerous jobs, like exploring volcanoes or putting out fires. Robots can also do repetitive stuff that needs to be done over and over again, like packing boxes or drilling holes.

The idea for machines to do this is very old. In the first century CE, an inventor called Heron, who lived in Alexandria, Egypt, was thinking of ways to make **mechanical** workers. He got the idea from his new invention, a simple kind of steam **engine**, which he thought could power an **automatic** blacksmith workshop, making metal objects. Even the metalworkers hammering and bending the metal would be steam-powered machines.

9

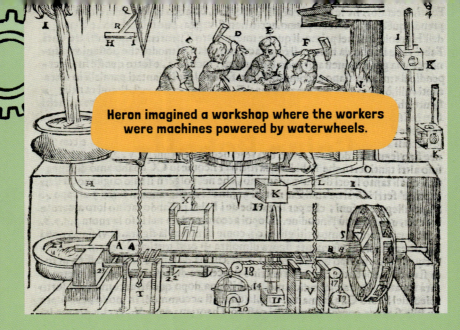

Heron imagined a workshop where the workers were machines powered by waterwheels.

Heron never put his ideas into action because the tools and technology he had could not do the job. We are much better at building robots today because inventors and **engineers** have spent 2,000 years figuring out how to do it. But we still have the same problem as Heron today:

how do we make robots that are smart enough to really be useful?

ROBOT HERO

Heron of Alexandria invented the first engine and imagined a factory run by robots.

GOING ROBOTIC

Automatic toys

About 1,000 years later, Ismail al-Jazari was an artist and inventor from what is now Syria who designed many amazing **automatons** and became known as the founder of robotics.

ROBOT HERO

Ismail al-Jazari built many elaborate robot-like machines that worked **automatically**.

Speak like a scientist

AUTOMATON

An automaton is a machine that repeats a set of movements over and over, working all by itself. A simple robot is a kind of automaton.

ROBOTS, GADGETS, AND ARTIFICIAL INTELLIGENCE

Al-Jazari's automatons were made from wood and powered by waterwheels that were hidden from view to make the motion seem more magical. The inventions were meant as toys, to delight his wealthy customers, but al-Jazari also made designs that replaced human workers. He built a mechanical servant that could **pour drinks for guests** and another that **flushed out water** for washing your hands and then **offered you a towel!**

Natural forms

In 1495, Leonardo da Vinci, who is most famous for his painting now called the *Mona Lisa,* created the Mechanical Knight. No one is sure if he ever built it, but the design was for an armored robot that moved all by itself. The great artist copied the structure of the human body to make the **mechanical joints**.

GOING ROBOTIC

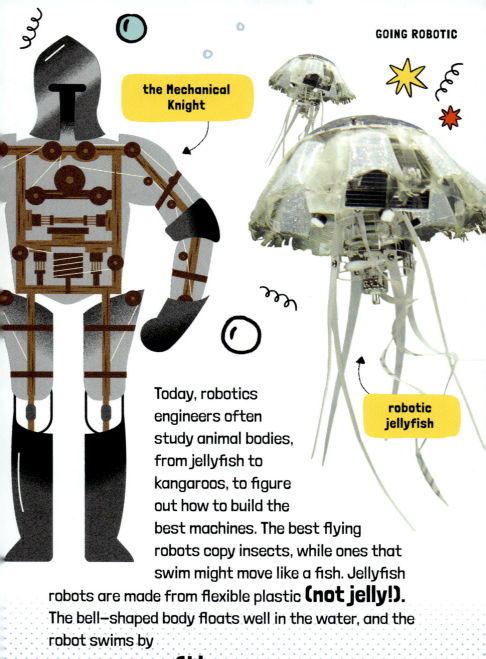

the Mechanical Knight

robotic jellyfish

Today, robotics engineers often study animal bodies, from jellyfish to kangaroos, to figure out how to build the best machines. The best flying robots copy insects, while ones that swim might move like a fish. Jellyfish robots are made from flexible plastic **(not jelly!)**. The bell-shaped body floats well in the water, and the robot swims by **wafting its long tentacles.**

ROBOTS, GADGETS, AND ARTIFICIAL INTELLIGENCE

The Digesting Duck, an automaton made in France in 1739, perhaps copied too much from nature. This copper bird could swallow grains of wheat, flap its wings, and then poop (made from breadcrumbs)!

Made from stories

The Steam Man was a robot designed to pull a cart—it didn't work, but inspired a **science fiction** novel called *The Steam Man of the Prairies.* Sometimes it works the other way around—technologies were invented in stories before they existed in real life. Characters talked to each other with small handheld gadgets in fiction long before smartphones became a normal part of everyday life. Robots were also well known in stories before they became a reality.

The idea of a robot appeared in a 1921 play by a Czech writer called Karel Capek. The robots in the play were not machines but **artificial** humans made from skin and bone. Capek created the new word **"robot"** for them because it was similar to the word for **"worker"** in the Czech language.

The Digesting Duck

GOING ROBOTIC

Capek's play created a craze for robots. In 1928, the British company Marconi built a robot called Eric. Eric was a metal human that could speak by transmitting a voice received via a radio connection. A few years later, a US company created Elektro, a six-foot tall metal robot that could walk, listen to spoken commands, and reply with recorded messages.

It even had a **pet robot dog called Sparko.**

Elektro

Sparko

That poop is NOT mine!

ROBOTS, GADGETS, AND ARTIFICIAL INTELLIGENCE

Frightening features

Early robots like Eric and Elektro were fun machines used to advertise the manufacturers at shows around the world. The people who saw them would have been reminded of other artificial humans from famous stories, such as the Tin Man from *The Wizard of Oz*, or Maria, a super-powered "machine person" from the science fiction film *Metropolis*.

GOING ROBOTIC

The stories about these artificial people do not always have a happy ending: the robots in Capek's famous play end up killing all the humans. The idea of a machine that looked and thought like people was pretty scary. Today, people still have worries about clever robots. Some are concerned that a robot will take their job and leave them with no way of making money. Others are scared that AIs will get so clever **that they'll take over the world,** like Capek's robots!

Another sci-fi author, Isaac Asimov, wrote about these kinds of worries in the 1950s. He included a set of rules in his stories—The Three Laws of Robotics—that would make it impossible for robots to turn on us.

The Three Laws of Robotics

 1. A robot may not hurt a human being or do nothing when a human being is about to get hurt.

 2. A robot must obey the orders given by humans except when that order means breaking the first law.

 3. A robot must protect itself from damage as long as that does not mean breaking the first or second law.

ROBOTS, GADGETS, AND ARTIFICIAL INTELLIGENCE

Asimov's laws show **us that humans** are always in charge of how a robot works. A robot will only become dangerous if we build it to do dangerous things.

Robot arms

The first robots built to do actual work were created about sixty-five years ago. They were simple robot arms that welded car parts in factories. This job is dangerous for humans because the hot welders give out poisonous fumes. Today, robot arms like this are still an important part of manufacturing in factories across the world.

A robot arm can be taught to move in a very exact way to do one job, and then taught another, and another.

The basic robot arm, called the Unimate, has **six "degrees of freedom."** This is another way of saying its jointed body can move back and forth in six separate motions, such as swiveling at the base, bending

18

GOING ROBOTIC

at the elbow, or opening its pincers. (The human body can do better than this: we have 230 degrees of freedom in all. Even the most flexible modern robots have some catching up to do.)

A robot arm learns its job by being moved by a human operator, like a dance teacher showing you each step in turn. The arm can then repeat the steps in the right order many times over, each time exactly the same as the last.

To do this, the robot needs three components: sensors, processors, and effectors.

SENSORS, PROCESSORS, AND EFFECTORS

This is the basic setup for all robots. The sensors in a robot arm pick up the motion of each joint, measuring how much each one moves and in which direction. The processor, which is a computer brain controlling the robot, stores that movement information. When it is time to get to work, the processor sends commands to the effectors. In the case of a robot arm, the effectors are electric motors that turn the wheel-like joints just the right amount to complete an exact movement.

ROBOTS, GADGETS, AND ARTIFICIAL INTELLIGENCE

Mechanisms and motors

A living body, like yours, also operates using the **sensor—processor—effector** system.

Your eyes (the sensor) see a ball above you.

Your brain (the processor) sends a message to your hand to catch it.

And your arm and finger muscles (the effectors) move to get the hand into the right position.

GOING ROBOTIC

Robotics engineers have invented sensors that can see better than our eyes, and processors that respond faster than our brains, but still, robotic effectors are no match for skin, bone, and muscle. While inventors are working on artificial versions of these materials, most robots are using the same simple mechanisms that al-Jazari would have known all about a thousand years ago—things like **wheels, screws, levers,** and **pulleys.**

Robotic motion generally comes from electric stepper motors. All electric motors work by using electricity to create strong magnets that **push and pull** on each other. Those forces make the motor spin around, and that turning motion might be used to bend a robot's arm or rotate its pincers. Stepper motors use at least four magnets to move the wheel in very precise ways, dividing up one complete turn into hundreds of tiny steps. This means robots are able to make very small and exact movements.

ROBOTS, GADGETS, AND ARTIFICIAL INTELLIGENCE

A simple **feedback loop** is used to make robot arms safe. If the arm senses an unexpected object blocking its path, then the processor stops the movements immediately.

Speak like a scientist

FEEDBACK LOOP

To make a robot smarter, engineers use a feedback system. The sensors check what the robot's effectors are doing and feed it back to the processor, creating a "feedback loop."

Our bodies are using **feedback** all the time, and to make better robots, engineers have to add in more and more feedback loops. For example, a robot that walks on legs uses feedback loops to stay balanced on rough ground. Feedback also helps a robot pick up an object without dropping it or crushing it.

GOING ROBOTIC

Better feedback can make robots become smarter and make fewer mistakes. However, adding more feedback loops makes the supply of information going to the processor very complicated. This makes it harder for the robotics engineers to create a clear set of instructions for the robot to follow. What is needed is a robot that can figure stuff out for itself.

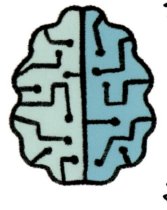

For that we need to give it **artificial intelligence, or AI.**

Chapter 3

What is AI?

We humans like to think we are the most intelligent animals on Earth. After all, which other animals build space rockets, cure deadly diseases, and share the latest memes? And which other animal has plans to build clever machines?

However, before we get too carried away with how advanced we are, we must not forget one thing: **humans still do not really understand our own intelligence.**

For example, how does the human brain work? How does it think, and where are our memories stored? And when we imagine a brand-new thing, where does that idea come from?

WHAT IS AI?

Types of intelligence

To build an artificial intelligence, inventors first have to figure out what intelligence actually is. And for that we can learn a lot from other animals. One way to understand intelligence is to divide it up into skills: movement, **perception**, attention, and knowledge.

The first one is movement, or "motor skill," which is how well an "intelligence" (a person, an animal, or perhaps a machine) can control its moving parts. An athlete or dancer has a very high level of motor skill but a robot arm in a car factory does not. The next ability is perception, or how well something can collect information from its surroundings. An eagle with sharp eyesight or a dog with excellent hearing both have better perception than any human.

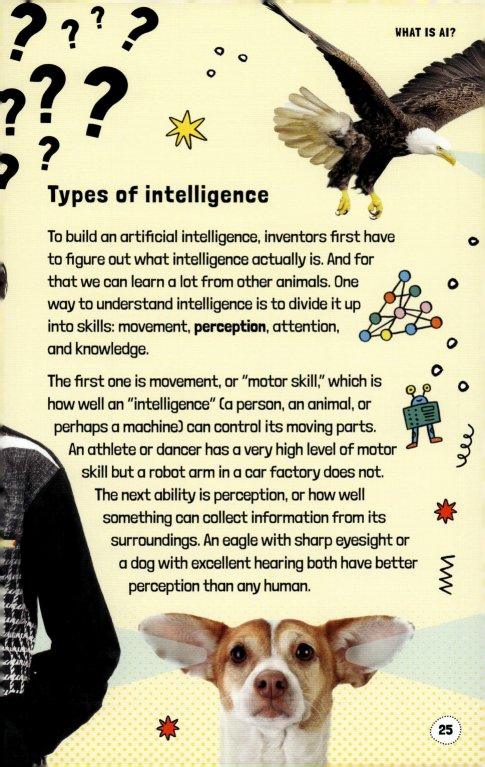

25

ROBOTS, GADGETS, AND ARTIFICIAL INTELLIGENCE

A computer might also have a sensitive microphone and camera that can pick up sounds and see things we cannot. Even so, the eagle, dog, or computer do not understand what they see and hear as well as a human might. For that they will need yet another kind of intelligence.

WHAT IS AI?

Memory system

The next skill is attention, or how long an intelligence can remember new information. There have been a lot of tests of a human's short-term memory. Lots of people can remember eight numbers or letters for about fifteen seconds. After that they start to forget them (repeating them restarts the memory clock, and stops people from forgetting). **Try it for yourself.**

People tend to focus their attention on one thing at a time. It is easy to imagine that a robot might be better at paying attention than us. It could receive and store information much more efficiently than our memories can.

The final intelligence skill is knowledge. This includes knowing how to count and do simple math, how to read and tell the time, plus all kinds of other facts about the world that mean the intelligent thing can understand what is going on right now—and perhaps figure out what will happen next. For example, a sharp-eyed eagle could see a flashing blue light from further away than you or I might, and a keen-eared dog would hear a siren wailing before we could. But only we might know what the blue light and siren actually mean: there is an emergency vehicle coming.

Let's get out of the way.

ROBOTS, GADGETS, AND ARTIFICIAL INTELLIGENCE

Humans are very knowledgeable. We start learning about the world as soon as we are born, and we get a lot of our knowledge by going to school as well as through play. In a way, AIs go to school as well—but they don't learn by playing like we do.

Testing intelligence

One way to make an artificial intelligence is to do what robotics engineers have done: copy nature. That means figuring out how a human, or any another animal, creates its intelligent skills. Then, it could be recreated using some kind of high technology, **such as a computer.**

WHAT IS AI?

This would mean the AI could work just like we do: thinking, dreaming, and imagining stuff. However, Alan Turing, who was one of the main inventors of modern computers, thought there was another way to make AI.

In 1936, Turing imagined a machine that followed a set of simple instructions to solve a problem. The imaginary machine helped Turing solve some complicated math, and he realized it could also be used to solve many different problems. Soon, Turing and others were building real versions of his machine, which became the first **electronic** computers.

Turing said it did not really matter **how** an **AI worked**, it just needed to **appear** to have the **same skills** as a **human**.

ROBOTS, GADGETS, AND ARTIFICIAL INTELLIGENCE

If it **appeared** to be a **clever, thinking machine**, then that is what it **was**—even if no one understood how it **actually** did it.

ROBOT HERO

Alan Turing was a leading figure in the science of computing, and he came up with the first description of AI.

Turing Test

In the 1950s, people were very excited about making giant artificial brains that could be as clever—or even cleverer—than people. That turned out to be much harder than anyone expected. We are still trying today! However, Alan Turing invented a test, called the Imitation Game (or **Turing Test**), that showed whether a computer was truly intelligent. The test is still carried out on today's AIs.

The game has two players. One of them is the computer AI, while the other is human. A second human acts as the judge. This judge cannot see the players but can talk to them by sending written questions.

WHAT IS AI?

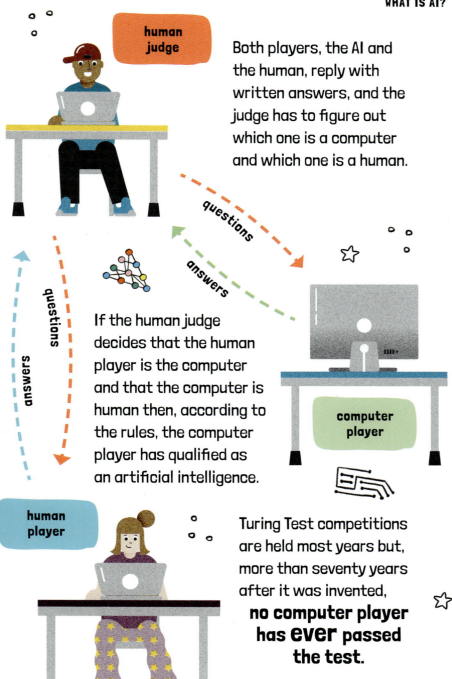

Both players, the AI and the human, reply with written answers, and the judge has to figure out which one is a computer and which one is a human.

If the human judge decides that the human player is the computer and that the computer is human then, according to the rules, the computer player has qualified as an artificial intelligence.

Turing Test competitions are held most years but, more than seventy years after it was invented, **no computer player has ever passed the test.**

ROBOTS, GADGETS, AND ARTIFICIAL INTELLIGENCE

The locked room

AI experts have pointed out that the Turing Test is not a perfect way of checking for artificial intelligence. Imagine that, instead of a computer, there is a human player locked inside a room, who cannot hear or see anything outside, and who receives coded messages from the judge. They can't read the code, but, there is a big code book that the human can use to look up the code symbols, so they can write a reply for the judge.

At no point does the person inside the room ever understand what any of the messages mean. In this way, the human mimics the computer because the computer program has to send out replies without understanding the question. If the code book is written correctly then the computer program can pass the Turing Test.

So this means the computer player is good at communicating, but is it really an artificial intelligence?

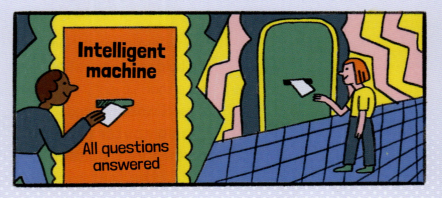

WHAT IS AI?

Perhaps we will know more once we've looked at how to make a real AI. Are you feeling ready for that?

Let's go!

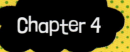

Chapter 4

How to Make AI

All artificial intelligence is created inside computers, and all computers are controlled by a program—a list of instructions and rules that the computer follows.

All programs have the same job: to turn **inputs** into **outputs**. An input is a signal that comes into the computer. That might be you typing some letters on a keyboard, talking into a microphone, or waving at a camera. Or it could be a long stream of information that measures something. For example, the input might be the number of cars waiting at traffic lights at different intersections around a city.

The program's instructions tell the computer what to do when it gets inputs. For example, when I press the Q key, these instructions result in an output, which is to make a Q appear on my screen.

HOW TO MAKE AI

The output from the traffic information might be to turn the lights to red at quiet intersections and to green at the busy ones, so more cars can get moving. The person who programs the system might have to create one set of instructions that works well in the morning, and a different set for the evening when everyone's going home.

Expect the unexpected

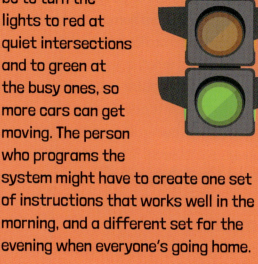

The programmer thinks up all the likely traffic problems and sets up rules and instructions to tackle them. But what happens if something unlikely and unexpected happens? **An elephant** is wandering along the main street and has blocked all the traffic. A human controller will have to take over from the computer because a human doesn't need pre-set rules to get the traffic flowing.

They look at the problem and figure out how to fix it using their natural intelligence. The human knows about the way traffic works—and the world in general. The computer program does not know anything; it just has a list of instructions to follow. The human controller can make up a new set of instructions to end the traffic jam, and this ability is what being intelligent really means. One way for a computer program to be an artificial intelligence is if it could write its own instructions and set its own rules, so that it could solve even unusual problems it's never seen before. **How could that happen?**

Inside a computer

To figure out how we might go about creating a computer program that could do this, we'll need to learn more about how computers work. All computers have three main parts: **input devices, output devices,** and **processors.**

A common input device is a keyboard, touchscreen, or game controller—anything used to send information and **commands** into the computer. We've come across

HOW TO MAKE AI

something similar with robots, which have **sensors** as their main input devices.

The most obvious computer output device is the screen, which is where we are most likely to see what the computer has done to the input—for example move the game **controller** and score a goal on the screen. Other output devices are **speakers** or **printers.** In a robot arm, the outputs are the actions of the effectors, such as an electric motor moving a joint or tools.

37

Microchips

The processor is the part that controls what everything else is doing. This is where the rules and instructions set out in a program are put to work. If we took a computer—or a robot—to pieces, the processor would be a small black square object we call a **microchip**. At its simplest, a microchip is a set of switches all connected by electric wires, but they are far too small to see without a powerful microscope. Today's microchips have many billions of these switches.

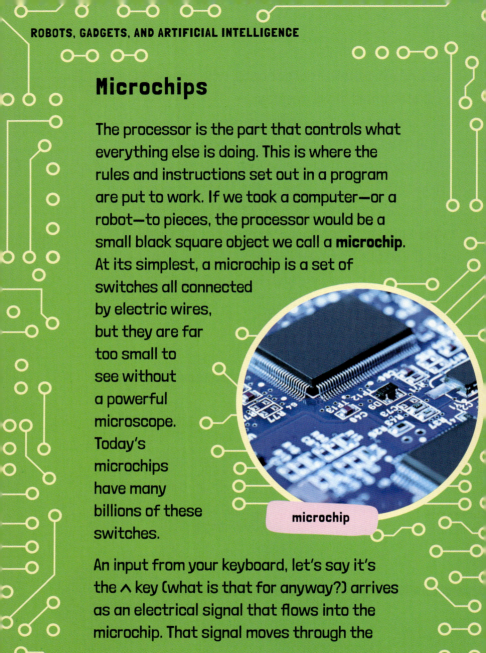

microchip

An input from your keyboard, let's say it's the ∧ key (what is that for anyway?) arrives as an electrical signal that flows into the microchip. That signal moves through the

HOW TO MAKE AI

maze of connections, following a particular path according to which switches are on and which ones are off. The electrical signal then leaves and travels to the computer's screen and a ∧ appears.

The switches in the microchip can flick **on and off many thousands of times a second,** and they do this according to the instructions set out by the program. So when you press the Q key, the input signal is different, and so the processor checks the program's instructions and turns it into a different output: Q.

Using codes

Computer programmers often call themselves "coders," and writing a computer program "coding." A human coder uses a programming language that is a mixture of words, symbols, and numbers.

What is 1.5 + 6.3?

```
NUM1 = 1.5
NUM2 = 6.3

SUM = NUM1 + NUM2

PRINT('THE SUM OF
{0} AND {1} IS {2}'.
FORMAT (NUM1, NUM2, SUM))
```

THE SUM OF 1.5 AND 6.3 IS 7.8

This is a way for us humans to organize our instructions clearly. This language is then converted into a code that the computer uses. The signals processed by a computer are in a **digital** code, which is made up entirely of just two numbers: 1s and 0s.

Speak like a scientist

DIGITAL CODE

A code is a way of turning a message into a form that only certain people—or certain things—can understand. A computer processor does not speak or read our language, so a program is written in a number code. Another word for number is digit, and number code is better described as digital code. Digital technology is technology that is controlled using number codes.

HOW TO MAKE AI

This simple-looking code can be used for many things, such as storing numbers or recording the different notes in a tune. The code controls the switches in the processor: every switch receives a signal from its neighbor, or it might get two signals at once. The neighbor sends a **"1"** signal with an electric current and a **"0"** signal is no current. The switch then makes a calculation with the **1**s and **0**s it receives and converts them into a new signal that it sends on to the next switch. The math only works with the numbers **1** and **0**, and every answer is either **1** or **0**.

> George Boole invented this type of **math** in **1854**, almost **100 years** before the **first digital computers** were built.

ROBOT HERO

George Boole invented the mathematical codes used in computers.

ROBOTS, GADGETS, AND ARTIFICIAL INTELLIGENCE

 ## Speak like a scientist

ALGORITHM

The math created by Boole can be used to answer simple questions so that the 1s and 0s in the code can be used as answers like "Yes" and "No," or "True" and "False." A computer program is a long list of these kinds of questions set out in a series of steps. This kind of list is called an **algorithm**.

Mathematicians were using algorithms centuries ago to help solve tricky problems—in fact, the word "algorithm" comes from a Persian mathematician who lived about 1,200 years ago. His name was Muhammad ibn Musa al-Khwarizmi, but in Europe his name was written as Algorithmi. Al-Khwarismi's books included clever new ways of doing math, and these kinds of ideas became known as algorithms.

ROBOT HERO

Al-Khwarismi is the Persian mathematician who gave his name to algorithms.

ROBOTS, GADGETS, AND ARTIFICIAL INTELLIGENCE

The laundry algorithm example asks a lot of **"if"** questions. Other algorithms ask other simple questions such as whether the number is higher or lower than a certain figure, or they might simply command that the next step is the opposite of the one before. The step-by-step instructions also have **loops,** where one step sends the process back to an earlier step. The laundry algorithm is designed to loop until you run out of laundry. There are similar, but much more intricate, algorithms working inside every **computer,** every **gaming console,** and every other **gadget.**

The first person to create an algorithm for a computer was the mathematician Ada Lovelace. She was friends with Charles Babbage, who designed a mechanical computer in 1837. His machine did not use microchips—they had not been invented—but worked using cogs and levers.

Charles Babbage's Difference Engine would have worked very well but it was too complex for him to build at the time.

44

HOW TO MAKE AI

ROBOT HERO

Ada Lovelace was the first coder, or computer progammer.

In 1842, Ada Lovelace set out a system for using Babbage's machine to do a very difficult kind of sum. Babbage never got to build his computer, but Lovelace's written instructions were the first ever computer program.

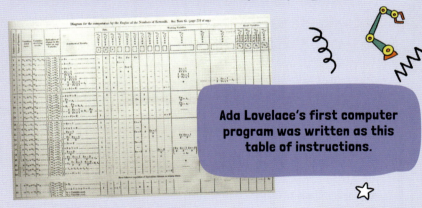

Ada Lovelace's first computer program was written as this table of instructions.

A learning machine

It is hard to imagine the laundry algorithm going wrong but the same is not true of a more complicated problem, such as managing the flow of traffic through the city. Let's think back to the **algorithm** that controls the traffic lights.

ROBOTS, GADGETS, AND ARTIFICIAL INTELLIGENCE

When this stops working properly, it requires a human intelligence to take over the controls. But no ordinary human can do it—a baby would be hopeless, as would you or I. The best person for the job would be a traffic expert who'd worked on similar problems many times before. They learn something new every time they tackle a new problem. The more they do it, the more they learn, and the smarter they get at keeping the traffic going.

What if we make an AI traffic controller using the same method? Instead of using a human to write the instructions, the program would figure out how to understand the traffic problem involving the elephant and write its own algorithm. And as it did its job more and more, it could rewrite and improve the algorithm.

✹ Speak like a scientist ✹

MACHINE LEARNING

AIs are often created using machine learning (or sometimes deep learning). This involves a special kind of processor called a neural network, which is made up of many layers sandwiched together. Each layer has many "nodes," or meeting points, and each node connects to every other node in the layers either side. The front layer's nodes receive input signals, which then move through the hidden layers until they arrive at one of the nodes on the back layer, and this is the output.

HOW TO MAKE AI

A computer program like this would appear to be just as intelligent as the human expert and do the job just as well—or maybe even better.

The neural network uses mathematics to guide an input through all the layers. At first all the answers from those calculations are wrong because it's just trial and error, so the network cannot turn an input into the right output. It needs to learn how to do that by comparing how wrong it was and trying again, and again. Eventually, after a long period of machine learning, the neural network has created an intelligent system that has been trained to do a job—perhaps to control traffic, or play chess, or recognize a picture of elephants . . . and there happens to be one on the next page.

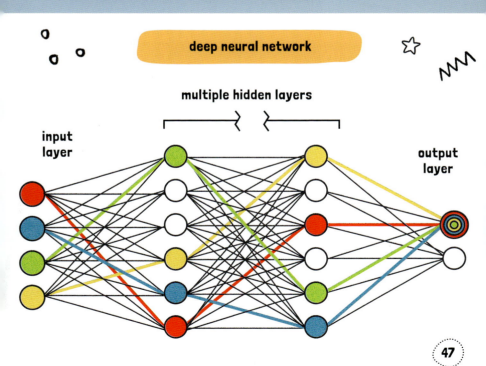

ROBOTS, GADGETS, AND ARTIFICIAL INTELLIGENCE

All pictures are a pattern of light and dark and different colors. A computer converts this pattern into a digital code. If the picture is of an elephant, then somewhere in that long string of 1s and 0s is an elephant pattern. We cannot see the pattern until the computer converts the code back into a picture on a screen or a printout.

> Once we can see it, we know immediately what that collection of **trunk**, **flappy ears**, and **long tusks** means: **elephant!**

Instead put this digital code into a neural network. It zings around inside and

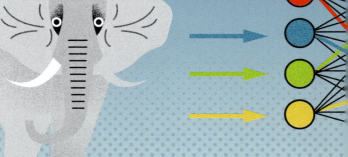

HOW TO MAKE AI

produces one of two outputs: "elephant" or "not elephant." To begin with, the network is making a **complete guess,** but it remembers if it gets it right or wrong. Now put in the code for another elephant picture, and another, and another, and keep going for thousands, even millions, of times.

Each time the network gets the **right answer,** it learns something new about how to recognize the pattern of an elephant in the code. It finds that codes that take a certain route between the nodes in its many layers are more likely to be elephant pictures. Codes that travel in other ways are not elephants.

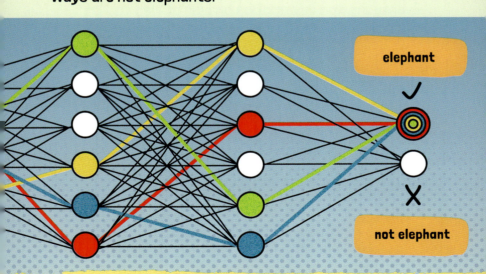

ROBOTS, GADGETS, AND ARTIFICIAL INTELLIGENCE

Clever classifier

A neural network is a way of classifying information that might, at first glance, look all jumbled up and confusing. Being able to sort things out into different types is an important part of being intelligent. For example, we sort out faces of friends from faces of strangers. We can even hear our name being shouted on a noisy street but ignore all the other sounds. AIs can filter out this kind of useful information using a system called a **decision tree**. You can imagine this as a tree with a thick trunk that splits into two branches, and those branches then split in two, over and over. A mixture of information comes into the "trunk" and is divided into two groups at each branch. Eventually, the information arrives at "leaves," at the end of the many branches, all sorted out into various types.

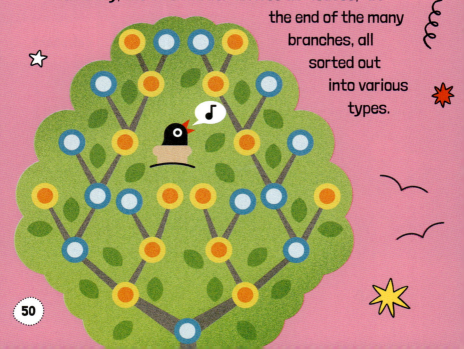

HOW TO MAKE AI

In a simple example, the input could be a mixture of circles and squares. The first branch sends the circles left and the squares right.

Next, the branch divides the shapes by size, so any squares or circles above a certain size go left, and below that size go right. After just two steps, the tree has sorted the mixture of inputs by size and shape.

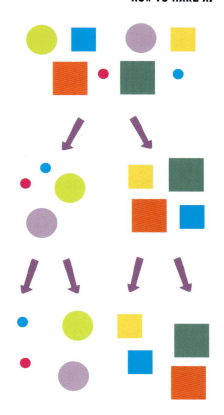

AI in action

If we can teach an AI to sort out shapes and see elephants, what other patterns could we ask it to look for? It could search for faces in crowds, or learn to recognize the sound of your voice, or even your smell! Maybe an AI could find patterns that we didn't even know were there? That really would be clever.

Now it's time to meet some superstar AIs that can do things no human has ever managed.

Chapter 5

Meet the AIs

It makes sense that we create artificial intelligence that looks for patterns, because we humans are very good at finding patterns in the world around us. Nevertheless, there is still more than one type of AI.

The elephant-scanning AI that we made in the last chapter—let's call it "ElephantFinder"—is described as a "**narrow AI**," or sometimes a "weak AI." A narrow AI is capable of doing one thing, or a few things. It may be able to do that job very well, but it still has only a narrow set of abilities. Just as importantly, ElephantFinder does not *know* that there is anything else to do other than look for elephants.

MEET THE AIS

Narrow and general

A narrow AI may be much better than a human at its one job, but it is still nowhere near as intelligent as a person—or any animal. A person has general intelligence, and so an AI that has a similar level of intelligence is called a "**general AI**," or sometimes a "strong AI." A general AI is clever enough to know that it does not know something, and it knows how to find out about it.

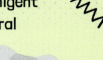

ElephantFinder does not see lions or tigers in pictures, it just sees "no elephants." It could, of course, learn to see big cats just like it did with elephants, but it cannot do that alone. Instead, a human controller must step in to direct its training—or perhaps a general AI could do that. So far, no programmer has ever managed to create a general AI. Maybe one day!

53

ROBOTS, GADGETS, AND ARTIFICIAL INTELLIGENCE

Being an expert

The third kind of AI is the "**expert system**," which is slightly different from the narrow and general types. An expert system has been programmed using human experts with all the patterns it needs to know. The AI compares the situation it's working on with all of the information stored in its memory. Once it finds a match, it knows what to do next.

A system used to figure out what illness a person has is a good example of an expert system: the patient answers questions that the expert system uses to figure out what might be wrong. This is more or less the

MEET THE AIS

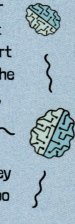

same as the way a human doctor diagnoses a patient. The doctor is an expert who knows what each answer means. Depending on each answer, they ask different questions until they get to a final **diagnosis**. The expert system does exactly the same thing, and as long as the human expert who came up with the program is right, then the expert system is right as well.

Expert systems are the simplest form of AI and so appeared first. Narrow AIs are harder to make but they are becoming very common now. A general AI is still too hard to build, but maybe **one day we'll make computers that are smarter than us!**

ROBOTS, GADGETS, AND ARTIFICIAL INTELLIGENCE

Deep Blue

There are different kinds of AI at work around us. Often, we have no idea they are there! However, there are a few AIs that are already famous. One of the first AI superstars was Deep Blue, a chess computer that played against the world's best human chess player in 1997.

Deep Blue was an expert system. Before taking on Garry Kasparov, the Russian world chess champion, its programmers loaded Deep Blue with every move of every game that Kasparov had ever played. They also added in many thousands of other games played by the best human players in history.

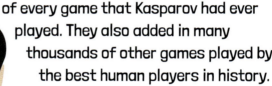

MR. KASPAROV

VS.

MR. DEEP BLUE

MEET THE AIS

As Kasparov made his moves, Deep Blue checked through its memory looking for games where the same thing had happened, and then looked up what the winning player had done in return. To do all this work, checking millions of options between every move, Deep Blue needed one of the biggest and fastest computers in the world at the time.

> **Deep Blue beat Kasparov!**

Watson

Deep Blue was built by the computer company IBM. In 2004, IBM built Watson, an AI that understood language spoken in a normal, natural way, just as we understand it. Watson was put to the test in 2011, when it was a contestant on the TV game show *Jeopardy!*, a general knowledge quiz.

Watson was up against the two best human *Jeopardy!* players, but still won. It helped that it could press the buzzer with a robotic finger much faster than the humans could, but it was also quicker and better at coming up with correct responses.

ROBOTS, GADGETS, AND ARTIFICIAL INTELLIGENCE

Nevertheless, Watson was a narrow AI. It had learned to recognize phrases and meanings of words. It used hundreds of different techniques to figure out the meanings for each quiz question. Some techniques came up with the same answers, and the most popular answer was the one Watson used—and it did all this in a few thousandths of a second. However, when Watson won the game and was awarded a **$1 million prize,** it was the only intelligence in the room that did not know it had won!

MEET THE AIS

AI in action

Narrow AIs like Watson are now common in everyday life. When you type a message on a smartphone, an AI is busy trying to predict what you are going to say. It suggests the words you probably need to help speed things up and sometimes this can be really annoying! A smart speaker, such as Alexa or Siri, is able to understand when you speak to it and carries out your requests. Play music! Search the internet! Do the grocery shopping!

Buy more ice cream? I did that yesterday!

The AI is not actually inside the speaker but is connected to it by the internet. So the AI is listening to millions of people all over the world talking in different languages. Now that really is **very smart!** Smart speakers do make mistakes, but every time we speak to one, its AI is getting smarter, using machine learning to get better at understanding us.

59

ROBOTS, GADGETS, AND ARTIFICIAL INTELLIGENCE

AlphaGo

One interesting AI is called AlphaGo, which was created by Google in 2014. It was given the job of learning *Go*, a board game from China, which is harder to figure out than chess in terms of computing power. In 2016, AlphaGo beat the South Korean player, Lee Sedol, who had been the *Go* world champion eighteen times.

MEET THE AIS

AlphaGo had several separate neural networks to learn how to play *Go* and used a math technique that comes up with ideas at random and compares them to figure out which is the best. After becoming the world's best *Go* player, AlphaGo then taught itself how to get even better at the game by playing itself over and over again.

Part of human intelligence comes from our sense of self, or the way we know that we exist. No one knows for sure where this sense comes from. One idea is that it just appears from the huge number of signals zinging around our brain. As AIs like AlphaGo continue teaching each other to become smarter and smarter, it is possible that an expert AI might become complex enough to get a sense of self in the same way and then become a general AI.

> Or it might **not** work like that at all!

A general AI would be very powerful, especially if it could make use of robotic technology and other gadgets to interact with us and the world. There is plenty of exciting tech out there.

Let's take a look at that next.

Chapter 6

Smart Robots and Clever Gadgets

Robots have got a lot smarter since the days of Eric, Elektro, and the Unimate robot arm from the 1960s.

There are robots that run on wheels and drive themselves—even on other planets! Flying robots, or **drones**, are very common, and there are even robots that can play tennis, clean up the house, and hold conversations.

SMART ROBOTS AND CLEVER GADGETS

One reason for this is an improvement in sensors and effectors. Sensors are the parts of the robot that first collect information about what is going on, and effectors move the robot's body in the right way in response. For example, NASA's Mars rovers, such as Perseverance, use a double set of video cameras to look out on the red planet, just like two eyes. The two cameras create a **3D** picture of the surface, so the rovers can see the shape, size, and distance of rocks clearly.

NASA's Mars rover

ROBOTS, GADGETS, AND ARTIFICIAL INTELLIGENCE

Meanwhile, robots have become stronger, more flexible, and more agile by using **hydraulic** joints. For example, the robot Atlas can walk, run, and jump on two legs like we do—and can even do handstands. It has no head, though—so it is easy to tell us apart—but does have arms for lifting things and opening doors. Atlas is still being tested and improved but something like it could be used for searching burning buildings or other places that are too dangerous for human rescuers.

Atlas

Atlas has a dog-like friend called Spot, which is already for sale—for $74,500. Spot is a good deal smarter than Sparko, the first robot dog in the 1930s. It is used by soldiers and rescue workers, and even performs in dance shows!

Spot

SMART ROBOTS AND CLEVER GADGETS

Self-driving cars

Robot brains, or processors, have also been given a big boost with more powerful microchips plus better programming, including AI. A good example of this clever computing in action is a driverless car, which is really a wheeled robot that you sit inside! (The first cars were called horseless carriages, so perhaps driverless cars will get a new name soon too.
What would be your suggestion?)

A driverless car's effectors are the same as those of a normal modern car. It might have a gas engine, but more likely an electric motor turns the wheels, plus there are brakes and a steering system (but maybe not a steering wheel). In place of the human driver, the car uses several sensors to figure out where it is, what route it should take, and when it is safe to stop and start.

The first sensor is a GPS system. This stands for Global Positioning System and is the same technology used by a maps app on a smartphone. The GPS talks to a fleet of satellites orbiting Earth to pinpoint almost exactly where the car is. The car's processor uses that to figure out the best route to take for its journey.

ROBOTS, GADGETS, AND ARTIFICIAL INTELLIGENCE

That's the easy bit. Next, the car needs to find out what is around it as it travels along the road. The car uses two types of sensor for this job. First, cameras point forward, back, and to the side to pick up the shapes of objects all around the car. An AI can detect patterns in these shapes and figure out which are other cars, and which are people, cyclists, road signs, road markings, objects, or animals in the road—maybe even an elephant.

emergency braking

pedestrian detection

collision avoidance

adaptive cruise control

SMART ROBOTS AND CLEVER GADGETS

Second, a **lidar** system shines an invisible laser around the vehicle and picks up any reflections. (Lidar is short for Light Detection and Ranging.) The lidar system tells the car's processor whether objects are moving or staying still, what direction they are moving in, and how fast.

The car's AI then puts all this information together to create an overview of the road and follows rules on how fast to go, when to change direction, what route to take, and when to stop and start.

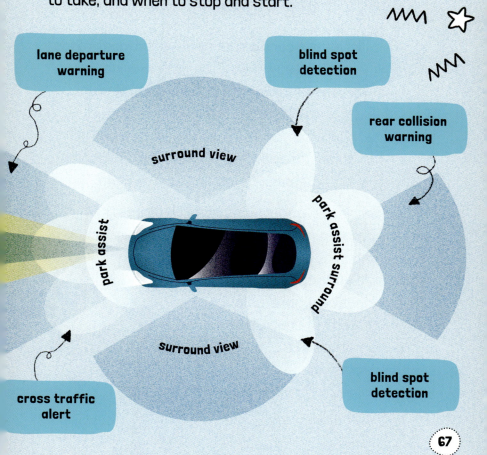

ROBOTS, GADGETS, AND ARTIFICIAL INTELLIGENCE

That sounds like it's a very big job, and it is—the car uses a powerful computer—but it's only what every human driver is doing all the time. Self-driving cars are still nowhere near as good as a human driver, but they are getting better all the time.

Robots meet humans

Driverless cars are not allowed on most roads yet, but many of the technologies they use are already at work inside cars with human drivers, helping to make driving safer and easier. Other types of robot technology are also being designed to work with humans, not in place of them.

For example, a robotic suit controlled by a person inside is called an **exoskeleton**, which can work in place of a body part. Someone might use an exoskeleton to help them walk. These kinds of robotic aids are still being tested but could soon provide more choice of equipment for disabled people.

SMART ROBOTS AND CLEVER GADGETS

Or an exoskeleton can make a human super strong. The human controller operates the suit by moving their arms and legs, and the exoskeleton's powerful robotic limbs copy the motion, but with much greater power and strength. Lightweight exoskeletons are being developed that make it easier to walk or run long distances without getting tired.

Exoskeletons can also be used as heavy-lifting machines in places where carts and trucks do not fit.

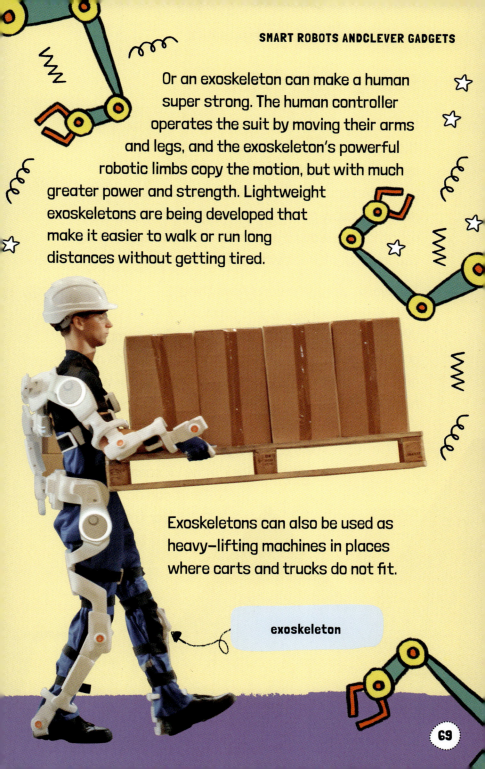

exoskeleton

ROBOTS, GADGETS, AND ARTIFICIAL INTELLIGENCE

Seeing and feeling

It is also possible to operate these powerful robotic devices by remote control, even from a great distance. To do this well, the human operator needs to know as much as possible about where the robot is. One way to do this is to use **virtual reality** technology, also known as VR.

The word "virtual" means something that seems real but is just an illusion. VR helmets hold screens in place and use computer graphics to create a 3D location to look at and move around in. Meanwhile, haptics (from the Greek work *haptikos*, which means "grasp") is the technology of touch. Haptic gloves squeeze the fingers, so it feels as if they are touching or holding objects inside the VR scene. A haptic suit can do the same for the whole body!

SMART ROBOTS AND CLEVER GADGETS

A VR version can be used to practice complicated tasks over and over, getting it just right before doing it for real. Surgeons do this when preparing for difficult surgeries.

heart

A human controller moving around a VR environment can control a robotic device that is far away in a real place. For example, an expert human doctor could **save the life** of a patient in another country by controlling a robotic surgeon using **VR.**

ROBOTS, GADGETS, AND ARTIFICIAL INTELLIGENCE

Telepresence

It might be that robots will help us travel without moving in future. This sounds more complicated than it is. Instead of catching the bus to the airport and then flying across the world to visit friends or meet for business, we could simply stay at home and hire a telepresence robot in the far-off country—much better for the environment.

At the moment, these robots are simply screens on tall stands that roll around on wheels. Using your home computer, you can control this telepresence robot as it trundles around a building, up and down the lift, and into and out of rooms. Everyone the robot meets sees your face on the screen and can hear

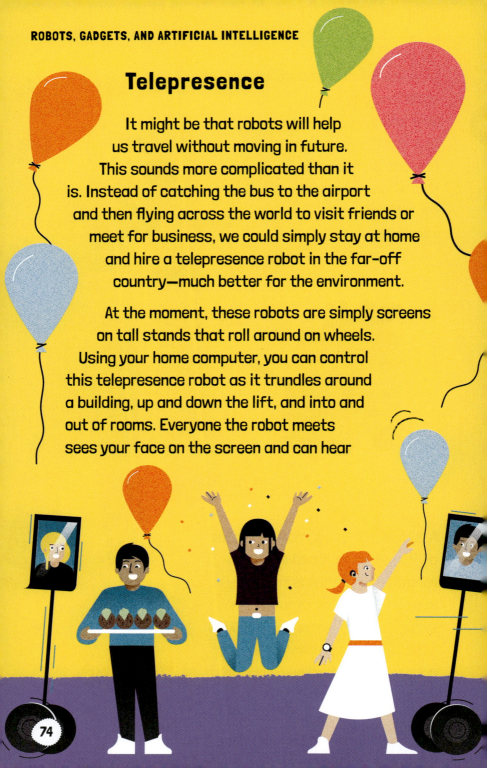

SMART ROBOTS AND CLEVER GADGETS

you talking. It's as if you were really there! In the future, VR tech and better, more agile robots might make this telepresence system work even better.

Robot to robot

An **autonomous** robot works without being controlled by a human. However, it is a big job for one robot to do all of its thinking by itself. Instead, robotics engineers can give their robots a connection to the internet. The robots can use that connection the same way humans use it. It can look up things that it needs, receive instructions or requests, and send out information about what it has been doing all day!

It is not just robots that are connecting to the internet, all kinds of machines are doing it—from fridges to cars to washing machines and even toys. When the internet was set up in 1969, it was created to connect computers together.

By the start of the twenty-first century, the internet had changed and was connecting people by sharing messages, videos, and photos. Now this "Internet of People" is transforming again into the "Internet of Things."

How would you feel meeting friends who were actually robots?

ROBOTS, GADGETS, AND ARTIFICIAL INTELLIGENCE

More than half the people on Earth—about 4 billion people—use the internet today, but already there are far more "things" with connections. By 2030, it is thought there will be at least 120 billion things on the internet. Those "things" will include robots, space rovers, delivery drones, cars, satellites that count icebergs, cameras watching for traffic jams, solar panels, smartphones, submarines, toasters, front doors, toilets, and perhaps even microchips embedded into our skin that check our health.

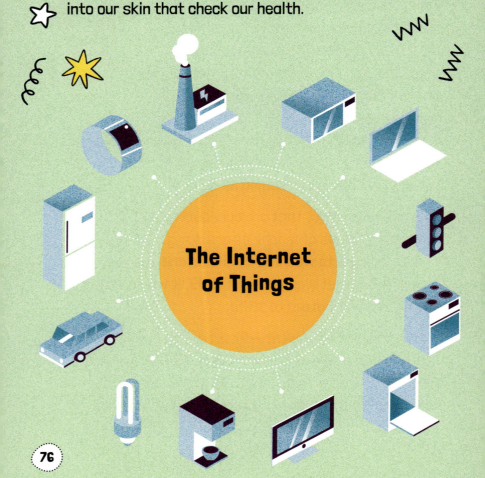

The Internet of Things

SMART ROBOTS AND CLEVER GADGETS

Speak like a scientist

VIRTUAL REALITY

The computer-generated simulation of a 3D image or environment, which people using special electronic equipment can interact with in a seemingly real or physical way. Equipment could be a helmet with a screen inside, or gloves fitted with sensors.

ROBOTS, GADGETS, AND ARTIFICIAL INTELLIGENCE

Virtual reality is very similar to systems used in computer games, and **VR gaming** is becoming more popular (although it might make you feel seasick!). VR can be used to control drones flying on the other side of the world or rovers rolling over another planet, in just the same way that a gamer moves through a fantasy world created inside a game console.

Gaming software creates virtual objects that have a particular size and shape, such as a soccer ball and goal, or monster alien or spaceship. As they play the game, gamers use controllers to move the objects around, and the computer has to figure out what they look like as the objects spin around, move further away, or are hidden behind other shapes. The same technology can be used to recreate a real place—like your bedroom or the surface of Mars—and once set up, you can move around it in VR as if it was the **real thing.**

SMART ROBOTS AND CLEVER GADGETS

The Internet of Things is not just a collection of connected gadgets, it also includes all the information that is sent and received by them. The number of messages sent to, from, and between things every day is enormous. By 2025, the Internet of Things had collected about **75 zettabytes** of data. That's 75,000,000,000,000,000,000,000 bytes—count all 21 zeros in that huge number!

Data is the name for information that has been collected. You can have data about anything: how tall people are, how old astronauts are, or what police officers eat for breakfast. A smartphone has room for about 36 million bytes, or 36 megabytes, of data, so we would need 2,000 trillion phones to store all this information, which is roughly 250,000 phones per person!

 Speak like a scientist

BIG DATA

Scientists call information gathered from the internet "Big Data." Big Data contains many interesting facts and patterns. For example, when people start shopping for certain medicines, this gives doctors a strong signal that an outbreak of an illness is about to happen.

ROBOTS, GADGETS, AND ARTIFICIAL INTELLIGENCE

Smart house

Big Data, the Internet of Things, and AI could work together to make houses smart. An AI will have control of everything: the lights, the air conditioning, the curtains, doors, oven, and fridge. It will use all kinds of Big Data such as the weather, how long you've slept, how busy you are at school, and what you've been eating. Then the AI will make your bedroom just the right temperature, cook you a meal you'll like, find a movie to watch or game to play, suggest you call a friend or get an early night. Do you think it would be nice to be looked after by an AI?

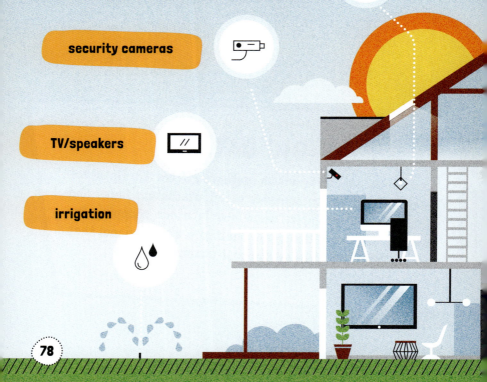

lighting

security cameras

TV/speakers

irrigation

SMART ROBOTS AND CLEVER GADGETS

This smart system can work on a bigger scale. An AI will one day be in control of the water supply, another will run a smart and very efficient electricity grid, and one more AI will manage the city's transport.

What if all these AIs shared their data to create a single super-smart system? Such an AI would be very powerful. Is that a good thing?

In the final chapter we'll take a look at how humans and technology might get along in the future.

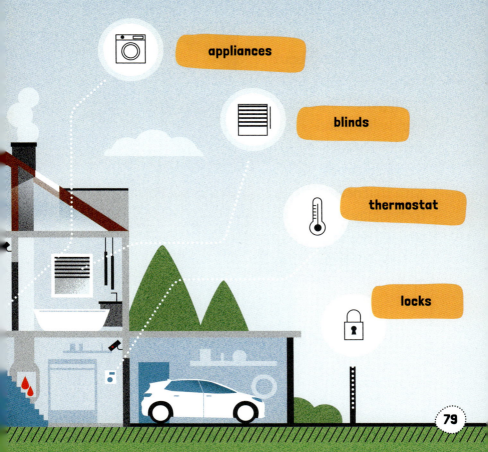

Chapter 7

AIs and Us

Every year, engineers, computer experts, and inventors are getting better at making robots and AIs. We are going to have to figure out how we live in a world where there are smart robots and smart computers working among us, doing things that people used to do.

How will we feel about living with these new intelligent things? A lot will depend on how we talk to and interact with this new technology and how we are able to take control of it.

AIS AND US

Simply smart

One of the first experiments into intelligent robots was carried out more than seventy years ago by an expert in the human brain called William Grey Walter. Walter created two simple wheeled robots, which he named Elmer and Elsie, to investigate how brains work, not how robots work . . . but in the end, he did both. Walter fitted Elmer and Elsie with light sensors and programmed them to drive toward light. The simple robots behaved very like animals, such as ants. They wandered around and then moved with purpose toward the light. Walter's experiments showed that even a very simple electronic brain, working all by itself, could do things that made the robots appear almost alive.

Elmer and Elsie looked a lot like turtles and simple devices like them are still described as turtle robots.

ROBOT HERO

William Grey Walter was a world leader in **cybernetics**, the study of how machines can be set up to be in control of themselves.

ROBOTS, GADGETS, AND ARTIFICIAL INTELLIGENCE

Being more human

Computers are not alive, as we know very well. However, when programming teams want to enter a Turing Test, which checks if a computer program has artificial intelligence, they create a **chatbot**, which is a computer program that can hold a conversation with the judge.

Chatbots are also used by call centers to answer simple questions and collect information. The best chatbots often make mistakes on purpose. For example, if the judge asks, "How are you?," the chatbot might reply, "I am verry well, thank you." The judge might think this misspelling is a mistake that a human would make and so decide that the chatbot is human—and that means it passes the test! Interestingly, it passes the test for getting something wrong and not for getting everything right.

AIS AND US

> Sounds too correct to be human!

Look-alikes

If we could build robot versions of ourselves, they would be able to do whatever work we can do—and much, much more. Perhaps we could be even be **friends!** Humanoids are robots that copy the human body. Humanoids are the hardest robots to build because they need to look and behave like us. If they don't get it right, we will definitely notice.

As well as communicating with words, people also say a lot with the expression on their face. We smile, frown, scowl, and stare to let people know what we are thinking. Kismet was one of the first robots to communicate with its face.

Kismet

ROBOTS, GADGETS, AND ARTIFICIAL INTELLIGENCE

Kismet had movable eyebrows, eyelids, and lips. Its programmer, Cynthia Breazeal, trained it to make expressions that would result in a human feeling protective toward it and acting kindly.

ROBOT HERO

Cynthia Breazeal is a leader in building friendly robots that can be used in the home.

The Uncanny Valley

The latest humanoids have hair, skin-like coverings over their mechanical parts, and are dressed in clothes to make them look more human. However, it often does not work. The more robots appear like real, living humans, the more we find them unsettling to look at— a strange effect known as the Uncanny Valley.

AIS AND US

It may be that robotics engineers can make humanoids so lifelike that we simply can't tell they are robots. It is likely that AI will help figure out that problem. Already, AI is able to change your face in very realistic ways in face-swapping apps and in **deepfake** videos. Even so, we are still really good at telling real faces from fake ones.

✳ Speak like a scientist ✳

DEEPFAKE

A fake video where an AI converts a photograph of someone into a video. It works by putting the face in the photograph on to the body of another person recorded in the original video.

ROBOTS, GADGETS, AND ARTIFICIAL INTELLIGENCE

Robot friends

Other robots are built to help us, so they are designed to appear cute and friendly. These kinds of robots are used as toys and teaching systems for children and as helpers in hospitals.

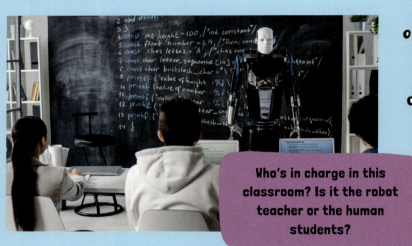

Who's in charge in this classroom? Is it the robot teacher or the human students?

There is also a robot astronaut called Cimon 2. It is part of the crew of the International Space Station and is designed to keep the human astronauts calm. Being a space robot floating in weightlessness, this little bot has no body. It is just a kind cartoon face that appears on a head-shaped screen and uses little fans to glide around inside the space station. Cimon 2 has the same AI used in Watson, the clever *Jeopardy!* winner. It chats to **astronauts**, helps them find **information,** and records the **results** of their **experiments.**

AIS AND US

This crew member's job is to make life easier for the crew, so they are less likely to get upset and make mistakes.

ROBOTS, GADGETS, AND ARTIFICIAL INTELLIGENCE

Future tech

There is a lot of uncertainty about the future of AI and robots. Some people worry that we will start to rely on these technologies too much and forget how to live without them. Others are concerned that a super-intelligent AI might form out of all the Big Data connected by the internet and take over the world! (And if it did, would we even know about it?) These sound more like science fiction than real life.

Computer experts are being very careful and discussing what AIs should be allowed to do—and what they should not.

AIS AND US

For example, in some countries an AI is not allowed to decide something for a human. When people ask to borrow money from a bank, the decision is normally made automatically by a computer. If a person does not like the answer, they are allowed to ask for a human to consider their application instead of the AI (hoping they will say yes). How this system will work as AIs are given more and more control still needs to be figured out.

One thing's for certain: **artificial intelligence** and **robot technology** is changing the world. It's going to be very exciting to see—and perhaps you'd like to be one of the inventors that makes it happen. **How smart would that be?**

Glossary

AI short for artificial intelligence; a smart computer program that allows machines to make decisions, solve problems, and do jobs that normally need a person

algorithm a set of instructions arranged in a specific order to solve a problem. Computer programs are made of algorithms

artificial something that is artificial has been made by people but often copies something that is natural

automatic something that works by itself, stopping and starting when it is needed

automaton a machine that repeats a set of movements over and over, working all by itself. A simple robot is a kind of automaton

autonomous able to operate without outside control

Big Data the huge amount of information collected from the many billions of gadgets connected to the internet

chatbot a computer program that holds conversations with people

code a way of converting information into numbers or symbols. Codes can be used for secret information or to convert information into a form that a computer or other machine can understand

cybernetics the science of how complicated mechanisms such as robots can be controlled

GLOSSARY

deepfake a fake video where an AI converts a photograph of someone into a video. It puts the face in the photograph onto the body of another person recorded in the original video

diagnosis identifying the source of a problem

digital to do with numbers, or digits

drone a flying robot that flies automatically, or an aircraft that does not have an onboard pilot and is controlled by remote control

effector the part of a robot that does things, such as motorized pincers and flashing lights

electronic technology based on electric currents that switch on and off in very particular ways. A computer uses electronics, as do most gadgets

engine a machine that burns a fuel and converts the heat given out into a movement

engineer a person that designs, builds, and fixes machinery

exoskeleton a rigid structure covering the outside of the body—insects have exoskeletons, and people can wear robotic exoskeletons

expert system a type of artificial intelligence that uses information from a human expert to figure out what to do

feedback loop a link between an output from a system and its inputs. A change in the output causes the input to be handled differently. Feedback loops allow the system to gather information about what it is doing, such as a robot arm knowing how it is moving or when it hits another object

GLOSSARY

gadget any small and useful device. A smartphone is a gadget

general AI a type of AI that knows that it does not know something. This kind of intelligence is more like our own. So far, no general AI has ever been made

hydraulic a hydraulic system is moved by pumping a liquid from one side to the other. The moving liquid pushes on a piston that connects to a movable joint, and the action of the piston makes the joint straighten or bend

inputs the signals or information that come into a computer or similar device

intelligence the ability to understand a situation as it is now, and decide what the best thing to do next is in order to achieve a goal

laser a focused beam of light or other radiation. Natural light is a mix of colors but lasers tend to be just one color (or perhaps two)

lidar short for Light Detection and Ranging, lidar uses invisible lasers to find objects nearby. The laser bounces back from the objects, and the lidar system uses the time it takes to come back to calculate how far away the object is

machine learning a way for a computer to program itself and write its own algorithm, and so become a kind of AI

mechanical describing a device that has moving parts. Robots are mechanical

microchip electronic device made up of billions of very tiny interconnected switches and other components

GLOSSARY

motor a device that creates motion from an electric current

narrow AI a type of artificial intelligence that can be very good at doing one job, such as recognizing faces or understanding voice commands, but is unable to do anything else. It is not even aware there is anything else that can be done. All AIs at work today are narrow

neural referring to the brain and nerves in animal bodies. A neural network device is organized a little like the nerves in a brain

outputs the signals that come out of a computer. An output might appear as a picture or word on a screen, a sound, or a printout

perception the ability to collect information from the outside world from sources such as sound, light, touch, and temperature

processor the part of an electronic device, such as a computer, that turns the inputs into outputs. The processor does this by using the instructions in a program

program the list of rules and instructions that allows a computer to process inputs into outputs

robot a complex machine able to work by itself to perform a number of jobs. The robot collects information from the outside world to figure out what to do and when to do it

robotics the science of designing, building, and using robots

science fiction a story in which characters use made-up technology that does not yet exist

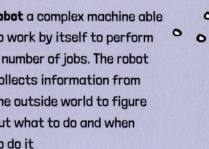

GLOSSARY

sensor a device that collects information from the outside world. Our body has many sensors, including the eyes and ears, and robots have similar artificial ones that see, hear, and sense the world

technology the use of the latest scientific knowledge to create new inventions

3D short for three dimensional, which means something has a length, width, and height—or at least, looks like it does. We see the world in 3D, which helps us see what is nearby and what is further in the distance

Turing Test one way of checking if a computer program is an artificial intelligence

Virtual reality (VR) computer-generated simulation of a three-dimensional image or environment that can be interacted with in a seemingly real or physical way by a person using special electronic equipment, such as a helmet with a screen inside or gloves fitted with sensors

Index

A
algorithm 42-47
al-Jazari, Ismail—see under **J**
al-Kwarismi, Muhammad ibn Musa
 —see under **K**
AlphaGo (AI) 60, 61
artificial intelligence / AI 6-8, 17,
 23-25, 28-34, 36, 46, 50-61,
 65-67, 78-80, 82, 85, 86, 88, 89
Asimov, Isaac 17, 18
Atlas (robot) 64
attention (type of intelligence)
 25, 27
automaton 11, 12, 14

B
Babbage, Charles 44, 45
Big Data 77, 78, 88
Boole, George 41, 42
Breazeal, Cynthia 84

C
Capek, Karel 14, 15, 17
chatbot 82
Cimon 2 (robot) 86
code 32, 33, 39-42, 48, 49
coder 39, 45
computer 6, 7, 19, 26, 28-32, 34-45,
 47, 48, 55-57, 68, 70-75, 80-82,
 88, 89
cybernetics 81

D
da Vinci, Leonardo 12
decision tree 50
Deep Blue (AI) 56, 57
deepfake 85
degrees of freedom 18, 19
Digesting Duck (robot) 14
digital code 40, 48
driverless car—see self-driving car

E
effector 19-22, 37, 63, 65
Elektro (robot) 15, 16, 62
Eric (robot) 15, 16, 62
exoskeleton 68, 69
expert system 54-56

F
feedback loop 22, 23

G
gadget 5, 7, 14, 44, 61, 62, 77
general AI 53, 55, 61
GPS 65

H
haptics 70
Heron of Alexandria 9, 10
humanoid 83-85

I
Imitation Game—see Turing Test
input 34, 37-39, 46, 47, 51
input device 36, 37
internet 8, 59, 75, 76, 88
Internet of Things 75-78

J
al-Jazari, Ismail 11, 12, 21

K
Kismet (robot) 83, 84
knowledge (type of intelligence)
 25, 27, 28
al-Kwarismi, Muhammad ibn Musa 42

L
lidar 67
Lovelace, Ada 44, 45

95

INDEX

M
machine learning 46, 47, 59
Mars rover 63
microchip 38, 39, 44, 65, 76
motor 6, 19-21, 37, 65
motor skill (type of intelligence) 25, 26

N
narrow AI 52, 53, 55, 58, 59
neural network 46-48, 50, 61
node 46, 49

O
output 34, 35, 37, 39, 46-48
output device 36, 37

P
perception (type of intelligence) 25, 26
processor 19-23, 36, 38-41, 46, 65, 67
program 6, 7, 32, 34, 36, 38-40, 42, 45-47, 55, 82

R
robot 6-19, 21-23, 25, 27, 37, 38, 62-65, 68-70, 73-76, 80, 81, 83-86, 88

S
self-driving car 65, 68
sensor 19-22, 37, 63, 65, 66, 71, 81
smart house 78
smart speaker 59
Sparko (robot) 15, 64
Spot (robot) 8, 64
steam engine 9
Steam Man (robot) 14

T
telepresence 74, 75
3D 63, 70, 71
Three Laws of Robotics 17
Turing, Alan 29, 30
Turing Test 30-32, 82

U
Unimate robot arm 18, 62

V
virtual reality / VR 70-73, 75

W
Walter, William Grey 81
Watson (AI) 57-59, 86

Introducing the AI experts:

AUTHOR

TOM JACKSON

Tom Jackson has been a writer for 25 years. He has written about 200 books and contributed to many more. He specializes in science and technology, and became a writer for technology magazines back when the world wide web was brand new. He now writes books for children and adults on all kinds of subjects, including engineering, computers, and technology. Today, Tom lives in Bristol, England, with his wife and three children, and can be found mostly in the attic.

CONSULTANT

DR. VAISHAK BELLE

Dr. Vaishak Belle is a member of faculty at the University of Edinburgh, and an Alan Turing Institute Faculty Fellow. He has co-authored over 70 scientific articles on artificial intelligence, and won best paper awards.

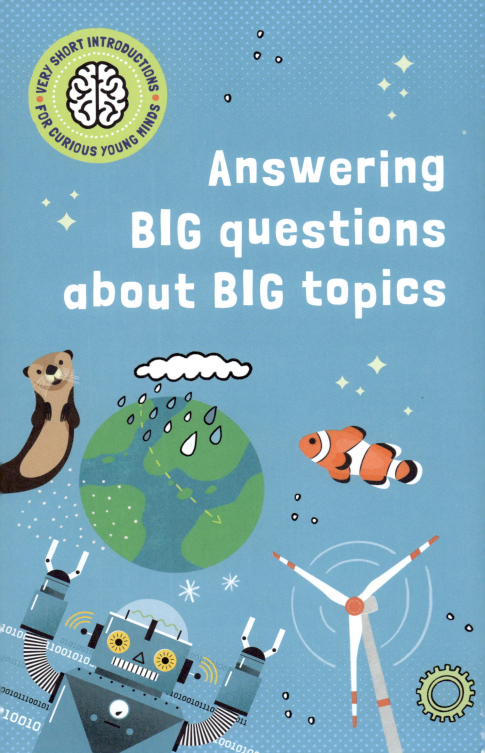